First Words!

By J. Douglas Lee

Pictures by David Mostyn

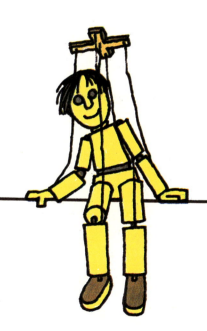

Gareth Stevens Publishing
Milwaukee

BRIGHT IDEA BOOKS:

First Words!
Picture Dictionary!
Opposites!
Sounds!

The Four Seasons!
Pets and Animal Friends!
The Age of Dinosaurs!
Baby Animals!

Mouse Count!
Time!
Animal ABC!
Animal 1*2*3!

Homes Then and Now!
Other People, Other Homes!

Library of Congress Cataloging-in-Publication Data

Lee, J. Douglas.
  First words!

  (Bright idea books)
  Bibliography: p.
  Includes index.
  Summary: Introduces over 250 words for familiar objects and concepts from home, school, and places of recreation. Special activities encourage readers to connect words in the text with objects in their environment.
  1. Vocabulary — Juvenile literature. [1. Vocabulary] I. Mostyn, David, ill. II. Title.
PE1449.L34   1985   428.1   85-25133
ISBN O-918831-86-5
ISBN O-918831-85-7 (lib. bdg.)

This North American edition first published in 1985 by

Gareth Stevens, Inc.
7221 West Green Tree Road   Milwaukee, WI 53223, USA

U.S. edition, this format, copyright © 1985
Supplementary text copyright © 1985 by Gareth Stevens, Inc.
Illustrations copyright © 1980 by Octopus Books Limited

First published in the United Kingdom with an original text copyright by Octopus Books Limited.

Typeset by Ries Graphics Ltd.
Series Editors: MaryLee Knowlton and Mark J. Sachner
Cover Design: Gary Moseley
Reading Consultant: Kathleen A. Brau

Contents

FIRST WORDS! 4
The Attic 4
The Zoo 6
The Kitchen 8
The Circus 10
The Supermarket 12
The Park 14
The Marina 16
The Toyshop 18
The Swimming Pool 20
The Soccer Match 22
The Moon Base 24
The Bedroom 26
The Workshop 28
The Playground 30
The Beach 32
The Hospital 34
The Pet Shop 36
The Restaurant 38
The Classroom 40
The Farmyard 42

Things to Talk About 44
Things to Do 44
First Words Index 46
More Books About Words 48

For Grown-ups 48

The Attic

skylight

feather

skis

telescope

dollhouse

doll

cobweg

spider

toboggan

hat

rocking horse

eyeglasses

album

trunk

The Zoo

zebra

kangaroo

cheetah   chimpanzee

peacock

giraffe

penguin

6

camel

lion

tiger

alligator

bear

elephant

7

door

apron

faucet

sink

refrigerator

chair

cat

recipe

cabinet

8

The Kitchen

paper towel

mug

tile

saucepan

stove

cup

coffee pot

iron

washing machine

ironing board

trapeze

acrobat

pony

bucket

11

cereal

honey

coffee

tea

sugar

orange

tomato

onion   potato

12

The Supermarket

clerk

candy

cash register

counter

milk

hot dogs

meat

cart

oak

kite

apple

bonfire

wheelbarrow

stroller

shovel

rake

lawn mower

swan

duck

petal

rose

15

cabin cruiser

deck

17

The Toyshop

jigsaw puzzle

tea set

cowboy

rag doll

package

baby carriage

record player

puppet

frisbee

records

soldier

counter

skateboard

19

lifeguard

snorkel

bathing suit

foot

hair

water wings

float

20

The Swimming Pool

window

tile

water

body

mouth

nose

hand

21

The Soccer Match

player

whistle

referee

goalpost

goalkeeper

camera

soccer ball

photographer

scarf

23

satellite

control tower

helmet

astronaut

24

The Moon Base

moon

nose cone

planet

spaceship

rocket

launch pad

25

The Bedroom

curtains

picture

mirror

pillow

carpet

slippers

blanket

lamp

dress

bathrobe

bed

socks

shoes

The Workshop

wire

flashlight

spring

ladder

paint

wood

pliers

ruler

saw

nails

hammer

drill

sawdust

railing

jeans

jungle gym

merry-go-round

slide

pocket

30

The Playground

puddle

umbrella

swings

seesaw

seagull

sandals

flag

pail

beach chair

sand castle

crab

seaweed

32

The Beach

ferry

goggles

skin diver

fisherman

pier

net

flippers

shell

pebble

33

blood

thermometer

patient

bandage

ointment

towel

34

The Hospital

doctor

soap

nurse

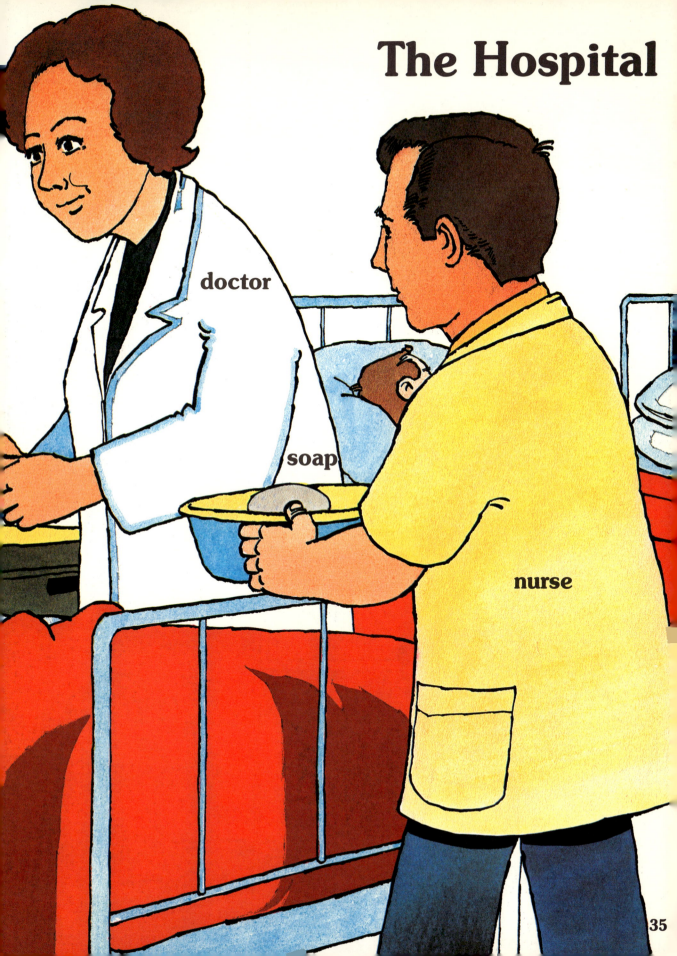

The Pet Shop

rabbit hutch

bird

kitten

puppy

rabbit

sacks

bird cage

snake

guinea pig

mouse

37

The Restaurant

sandwiches

waitress

juice

plate

glasses

38

light

ice cream
spoon

knife

fork

salad

placemat

bowl

soda

tablecloth

chair

ABCDEFGHIJKL MNOPQRSTUVW XYZ abcdefghijklmn opqrstuvwxyz

alphabet

book

ribbon

clay

stool

table

40

The Classroom

teacher

scissors

paste

pencil

painting

paper

The Farmyard

harvester

shed

wheel

headlight

shovel

tractor

hen

egg

42

field

gate

fence

farmer

boots

pond

pig

straw

43

Things to Talk About

The following "Things to Talk About," "Things to Do,"
and "First Words Index" sections offer grown-ups
suggestions for further activities and ideas to share with
young readers of *First Words!*

1. Find the picture of the zoo. Which animals can you
    find <u>outside</u> of a zoo? Where would you be able to
    find <u>them?</u>

2. Find the pictures of the Swimming Pool and the
    Beach. Which things at the beach could you find at
    the pool? Which things at the beach would you
    <u>never</u> find at the pool? Why not?

Things to Do

1. Use the table of contents or First Words Index to find
    the pictures of the Attic, the Kitchen, and the
    Bedroom. How many of the things that are named
    in these pictures can you find in <u>your</u> home? Ask a
    grown-up to help you write the names of certain
    things in your home on pieces of sticky paper. Then
    stick the papers on those things. Then you can read
    the names every time you see them in your home!

2. Ask a grown-up you know for a pencil and some
    tracing paper. Use the table of contents or Index to
    find these pictures in the book and trace them onto
    your paper:

    *the <u>fan</u> waving the <u>flag</u> at the Soccer Match
    *the <u>astronaut</u> wearing a <u>helmet</u> at the Moon Base
    *the <u>girl</u> in the <u>bathing suit</u> at the Swimming Pool
    *the <u>doctor</u> at the Hospital

    There are many things you can do with your
    drawings. You can color them with crayons right on
    the tracing paper. Or you can look at them very
    carefully and copy them onto thicker paper.

3. Here are two scrambled lists of things you can find in this book. Each word on the left has a matching word on the right that describes something very much like the word on the left. On a separate piece of paper, match each word on the left with the correct word on the right. If you don't know what a word means, you might ask a grown-up to help you. You might also use the Index on pages 46 and 47 to help you look up the words and find out what they mean.

pail	door
baby carriage	mug
goggles	puddle
pier	stroller
pond	eyeglasses
gate	bucket
cup	dock

4. Here are two more scrambled lists of things that go together. You can find all of them in this book. On the left is a list of bigger things. On the right are smaller things that go with the bigger ones. On a separate piece of paper, match each bigger thing with the smaller thing that goes with it.

Bigger than	Smaller than
bed	camera
referee	faucet
sink	petal
photographer	pillow
jeans	pocket
hammer	nails
yacht	whistle
flower	sail

First Words Index

A
Acorn 14
Acrobat 10
Album 4
Alligator 6
Alphabet 40
Ant 14
Apple 14
Apron 8
Astronaut 24
Attic, The 4

B
Baby carriage 18
Balloon 10
Bandage 34
Bathing suit 20
Bathrobe 26
Beach, The 32
Beach chair 32
Bear 6
Bed 26
Bedroom, The 26
Bee 14
Bird 36
Bird cage 36
Blanket 26
Blood 34
Body 20
Bonfire 14
Book 40
Boots 42
Bowl 38
Bucket 10
Buoy 16

C
Cabin cruiser 16
Cabinet 8
Camel 6
Camera 22
Candy 12
Carpet 26
Cart 12
Cash register 12
Cat 8

Cereal 12
Chair 8, 38
Cheetah 6
Chimpanzee 6
Circus, The 10
Classroom, The 40
Clay 40
Clerk 12
Clown 10
Cobweb 4
Coffee 12
Coffee pot 8
Control tower 24
Counter 12, 18
Cowboy 18
Crab 32
Crowd 22
Cup 8
Curtains 26

D
Deck 16
Dinghy 16
Dock 16
Doctor 34
Dog 14
Doll 4
Dollhouse 4
Door 8
Dress 26
Drill 28
Duck 14

E
Egg 42
Elephant 6
Eyeglasses 4

F
Fans 22
Farmer 42
Farmyard, The 42
Faucet 8
Feather 4
Fence 42
Ferry 32

Ferry boat 16
Field 42
Fire eater 10
Fisherman 32
Flag 22, 32
Flashlight 28
Flippers 32
Float 20
Flower 14
Foot 20
Fork 38
Frisbee 18

G
Garbage can 14
Gate 42
Giraffe 6
Glasses 38
Goalkeeper 22
Goalpost 22
Goggles 32
Greenhouse 14
Guinea pig 36

H
Hair 20
Hammer 28
Hand 20
Harvester 42
Hat 4
Headlight 42
Helmet 24
Hen 42
Honey 12
Hospital, The 34
Hot dogs 12

I
Ice cream 38
Iron 8
Ironing board 8

J
Jeans 30
Jetty 16
Jigsaw puzzle 18

Juggler 10
Juice 38
Jungle gym 30

K
Kangaroo 6
Key 4
Kitchen, The 8
Kite 14
Kitten 36
Knife 38

L
Ladder 28
Lamp 26
Launch pad 24
Lawn mower 14
Lifeguard 20
Light 38
Linesman 22
Lion 6

M
Marina, The 16
Mast 16
Meat 12
Merry-go-round 30
Milk 12
Mirror 26
Moon Base, The 24
Mouse 36
Mouth 20
Mug 8

N
Nails 28
Net 32
Nose 20
Nose cone 24
Nurse 34

O
Oak 14
Oar 16
Ointment 34
Onion 12

Orange 12
Orchard 14

P
Package 18
Pail 32
Paint 28
Painting 40
Paper 40
Paper towel 8
Park, The 14
Paste 40
Patient 34
Peacock 6
Pebble 32
Pencil 40
Penguin 6
Pet Shop, The 36
Petal 14
Photographer 22
Picnic 14
Picture 26
Pier 32
Pig 42
Pigeon 14
Pillow 26
Placemat 38
Planet 24
Plate 38
Player 22
Playground, The 30
Pliers 28
Pocket 30
Pond 14, 42
Pony 10
Pool 20
Potato 12
Program 22
Puddle 30
Puppet 18
Puppy 36

R
Rabbit 36
Rabbit hutch 36

Rag doll 18
Railing 30
Rake 14
Recipe 8
Record player 18
Records 18
Referee 22
Refrigerator 8
Restaurant, The 38
Ribbon 40
Rocket 24
Rocking horse 4
Rose 14
Rowboat 16
Rudder 16
Ruler 28

S
Sacks 36
Sail 16
Sailor 16
Salad 38
Sand castle 32
Sandals 32
Sandwiches 38
Satellite 24
Saucepan 8
Saw 28
Sawdust 28
Scarf 22
Scissors 40
Seagull 32
Seaweed 32
Seesaw 30
Shed 42
Shell 32
Shoes 26
Shop 36
Shovel 14, 42
Sink 8
Skateboard 18
Skin diver 32
Skis 4
Skylight 4
Slide 30
Slippers 26

Snake 36
Snorkel 20
Soap 34
Soccer ball 22
Soccer Match, The 22
Socks 26
Soda 38
Soldier 18
Spaceship 24
Spider 4
Spoon 38
Spring 28
Squirrel 14
Stool 40
Stove 8
Straw 42
Stroller 14
Sugar 12
Supermarket, The 12
Swan 14
Swimming Pool, The 20
Swings 30

T
Table 40
Tablecloth 38
Tea 12
Tea set 18
Teacher 40
Telescope 4
Tent 10
Thermometer 34
Tiger 6
Tile 8, 20
Toboggan 4
Tomato 12
Towel 34
Toyshop, The 18
Tractor 42
Trapeze 10
Tree 14
Trunk 4

U
Umbrella 30

W
Waitress 38
Washing machine 8
Water 20
Water wings 20
Wheel 42
Wheelbarrow 14
Whistle 22
Window 20
Wire 28
Wood 28
Workshop, The 28

Y
Yacht 16

Z
Zebra 6
Zoo, The 6

More Books About Words

Here are some more books about words. Look at the list. If you see any books you would like to read, see if your library or bookstore has them.

ABC of Cars and Trucks. Alexander (Doubleday)
ABC of Children's Names. Ewen (Green Tiger Press)
A, B, See. Hoban (Greenwillow)
All Butterflies: An ABC. Brown (Atheneum)
Animal ABC! Lee (Gareth Stevens)
*Animal 1*2*3!* Lee (Gareth Stevens)
Christmas Alphabet Book. Whitehead (Troll)
Farmer's Alphabet. Azarian (Godine)
Find Your ABC. Scarry (Random House)
Guinea Pig ABC. Duke (Dial)
My Word Book. Grosset & Dunlap (Grosset & Dunlap)
Opposites! Lee (Gareth Stevens)
Perfect Speller (How to Spell It). Greisman and Wittels (Grosset & Dunlap)
Picture Dictionary! Lee (Gareth Stevens)
Sounds! Lee (Gareth Stevens)

For Grown-ups

First Words! is a picture book that introduces young readers to over 250 words. The "First Words Index" is, in effect, a controlled vocabulary list of every term that is used in the main text (pages 4-43) of this book. The index will give educators, librarians, and parents a quick guide to using this book to complement and challenge a young reader's growing vocabulary.

The editors invite interested adults to examine the grade level estimate below. Certain books lend themselves to reading level analyses using standard reading tests. *First Words!*, because of its format, does not. This concept book helps children discriminate among objects by size, color, shape, and setting. The reading level of *First Words!* is therefore determined not only by how "hard" the words are, but by a child's ability to grasp the subject matter in a visual setting.

The grade level span given below reflects our critical judgment about the appropriate level at which children find the subject matter an achievable challenge.

Estimated reading level: Grade level 1-3